THE MIGHT

OF

LOVE

Copyright © translation from Bulgarian:
Darin Stoytchev

Second Edition, Paperback – published 2013

ISBN: 978-0-9667951-2-7

E-mail: themightoflove@gmail.com

Printed in Santa Monica CA U.S.A

FOREWORD

Put Love to be an engine of your thoughts, feelings, and deeds in order to succeed in your good wishes. Make small experiments with applying Love to try out the powers and possibilities that are hidden in it. Making small experiments, not big, produces great incentive in you. Sow a kernel of wheat and you will reap 30, 60, and more bushels of wheat. Everyone bears untold riches in his beautiful soul. If you don't use the Love key to reveal them and become rich, you bear the responsibility for that.

The Master says, "Say one good, gentle word to the man and God's blessing will begin to flow." Do a little good for somebody every day, thus you let Love flow through you. When you become a conductor of Love you help first yourself. (Most of the thoughts in the Foreword are also by Beinsa Douno/Peter Deunov, though not taken word for word; some sentences are with minor changes.) If you like this book you may want to check the books "Love Wisdom Truth", and "Prayers and Spiritual Formulas" as well. This book together with "Love Wisdom Truth", and "Prayers and Spiritual Formulas" are available for free (digital format). To get a free copy of the e-books send an email to: mainpem@gmail.com.

Enjoy your reading. Peace, Love, and Light.

Darin Stoytchev

In Love, in the Divine world, everything is positive.

People who have Love can be contented with just a little.

He, who loves, gives the way to the God in himself.

Outside of Love everything is a lie.

Love penetrates all of existence.

People talk about Love but still suffer.

Discontentedness, illnesses, and hate - show that you are outside of Love.

Love must be applied, not just extolled.
If your heart doesn't beat with love it is worth nothing.

Love must permeate in your subconscious.
Only in Love there is life.

Love for God and love for your neighbor are the two great laws that rule the world.

Love radiates lofty life.

One's face shows how much love is in it.
Love is serving the Lord.

Love is higher than any thought.

With Love everything vibrates with life.
Love is a stream of light.

If you think about Love, you'll attract its light.

When one loses Love, then the dissatisfaction comes.

Love is the greatest superiority.

Love never fails - only you may fail.

Only through Love can you think correctly.

God can only be known with love.

He who comprehends Love lives, but he who doesn't, ponders.

The evildoers become tortured when Love is spoken about.

Peace is based on Love.

Love and reason penetrate the whole universe.

Through Love one's deeds elevate.

For the man who doesn't believe in Love, there is no use for him to ponder.

If you start loving evil, it will change its relations with you.

Love melts the problems.

Only Love makes the man happy.

God has brought in Love for solving all problems.

Law: - Human love always ends with unhappiness.

Only Divine Love reveals the secret wisdom.

If you have Love, the paradise is in you.

Feed yourself with Love - acquire it from everywhere.

Love is a way through which God shows Himself.

Love defeats everything.

Only he who loves sees God.

The Divine science is a science of Love.

Crimes occur where Love and reason are weak.
Behind Love stands God's strength.

Love attracts all powers of the universe.

Whatever Love says, happens; that is the
strength.

Love is the support of the universe.

Only deep and pure Love reveals God's secrets.

Mark: The man of Love is pleased with
everything.

People will suffer until they comprehend Love.

Only Love appreciates all things.
Only that thing which is clean love will enter
God's kingdom.

Evil flees from Love.

Universe love is the secret of peacefulness.

Love and profound peace are inseparable.

All love belongs to God, not to man.

If somebody loves you - God loves you.

If nobody loves you, the reason lies in you.

Love which doesn't give meaning to life is a transient love.

Peacefulness exists only in Love.

Only Love thinks correctly. Every thought about Love is equal to light.

Where Love is, is where every negative thing retreats.

Knowledge comes from Love. The people of Love are always kind/noble.

Love is impossible to express.

Outside of Love a man will have bad opinion for the world

Love was born before the world was.

Patience is a quality of Love.

God created Love for connection with Him. Where there is love, there God acts.

Love governs everything and everyone submits to it.

Outside of the realm of Love things are meaningless.
Where Love is - there the devil trembles.

When you enter with love, you infect everyone with it.

When you act with love, Divine energies start flowing.

If Love leaves you, God has left you.

Only love towards God melts away Karma.

For Love everything is beautiful and light.

He who loves God will have everything.

Love is a universal force.
Only the clean heart has love.

Only Love can create a true man.

He, who loves only, has will.

The salvation of man doesn't lie in a church, but in Love.

When you lose Love, then comes the criticism.

Love produces the most beautiful life.

Emptiness is in those, who have no love.

Anything that is out of the realm of love is not real.

Have love towards your fate and it will improve.

Love creates a Divine atmosphere.

Love, Wisdom, and Truth – these are the greatest powers in the universe.

When Love enters man, it improves everything.

Humbleness is an expression of love to the Eternal.

Closeness among people depends on the love they have.

Happy people are people who appreciate Love.

Love, this is the rays of the light.
Who loves you? - He who brings in morals and life in you.

Law: If you love somebody he loves you too.

The Love doesn't belong to man.

"Love" is blind, but its marriage gives its eyesight back.

Only that which has happened with love will remain.

It's a great benefit to have the love of a man.

The best medicine is Love.

First Love –afterward, everything else comes.

When Love permeates deeply into the man he becomes rich.

If you don't love people you destroy yourself.

Cruelty - means denying Love.

Love breaks down all chains.

Love is the awakening of the supreme in man.

All benefits are nothing before Love.

Only Love can create true life.

Love to God must be stronger then the love to people.

The human love brings death, but the Divine brings life.

Love is a passport for coming back to the paradise.
Only Love carries in itself the truth.

Love is a holy science for all the times.

Love converts death into immortality.

Inside Love you are protected.

Through Love you enter to another world.

When Love enters in man - the unclean spirits exit out of him.

With Love the air is full of vital energy.

One can be without religion and church, but without Love, one cannot be.

Love is a mighty alchemy.

When the world disappears - Love will continue its existence.

The only world that can never be destroyed is Love.

9

When somebody loves you, he lives in you.

So as to understand Love, you must be into it.

Love has the thoughts and the feelings of God.

Love is woven of sun rays.

Love is the best life.

Philosophy is outer wisdom, religion is inner wisdom, Love is Divine wisdom.

Love has universal seeing.

In Love there is hidden and dynamic light.

A bad attitude to Love is a catastrophe.

Without Love the life quickly sets.

He, who doesn't appreciate Love, loses it.

Where Love dies, there the desert comes to birth.

Love illuminates it.

Mind and heart are enlightened only by Love.

Love is the foundation of space.

Without love, the mind fails and the heart gets damaged.

He, who lives in Love, reigns.
Good character comes from Love, but bad character comes from hate.

True love seeks first the glory of God.

Only Love builds character.

He who has Love - the truth comes to him.

Humbleness is the foundation of Love.

Love satisfies the mind and heart.

The only lasting love is God's Love.

Man is dissatisfied because he doesn't develop Love in himself.

Love possesses a bright mind.

Human love can't cope with the sufferings.

That thing that disappears and dries up is not love.

Inside Love, life is eternal.

When you are in the Divine Love, you do not dream - but live.

Love is a law for gaining eternal life.
The genuine inner love attracts everyone.

Love is a high world - therefore it can't be expressed.

The basic life law is Love.

The greatest thing for the man is to know Love.

He who is loved can't die.

Love exists only in the Divine world.

When Love leaves the body it is finished.

Love is a spiritual essence.

Love exalts and illuminates the cells.

Love is not a human sense, but it is a Divine one.

God is Love's spring, Love is known only through belief.

Only in Love you are full of life.

Only Love waters the mind and heart with life.

Criticism, hate, envy - they drive away the Love.

If your mind and your heart are tight, you receive nothing from Love.
If you are lightened up by Love, you'll burn forever.

Love brings the eternal goodness to mankind.

Love: that is the height of the soul.

Love drives away all dark powers.

When you master Love - death is helpless.

If you have love - you have the most important thing.

For Love, nothing is trivial and insignificant.

There is no born man who can describe Love.

When you lose Love you lose your mind and heart.

You are unhappy because the people love you - but not Love.

Love is a power that never loses.

Love without doubt is a great love.

Seek the inner love, but not the outer.
Love is the most beautiful world - in it resides
God himself.

Love to God is the center of life.

Real knowledge is that knowledge that is
acquired with love.

God relates to everyone with love.

Without love, the words are feeble.

If Love does not visit the cells - they become
unbalanced.

Love is full of goodness and prana.

All people who are forsaken by Love go to hell.

Love is a spiritual light.

There is calmness only in people soaked with
love.

Love gives away life.
Who knows Love? - He who has it in himself.

Any help comes from Love.

He who has no love is condemned.

All the laws are submitted to Love.
Love is above every religion.

The most safe place is God's Love.

God is visible in deep love and belief.

Love comes in among people in an invisible way.

That thing, that you seek, you can find in Love
only.

Love directs the people's favor towards you.

Hold the air a long time with love in yourself.

Love is blind to the people's mistakes.

Love is a full harmony between one
consciousness and another.

He who has love doesn't need laws.

Laws are for those who have no love and break
them.

Love visits only people who understand it.

God presents Himself as love in man.

Love is fullness; with it everything is achievable.

No matter how long you arrange your
businesses - without love nothing can be done.
Love visits only the man of the truth.
Only Love can endure the inner life.

Love flows out of God.

When you are loved, you perceive the
Divine Love.

Human love empties the mind, heart, and soul.

Only through Love things become clear.

Love leads people to God.

Inside God's love is immortality.

Love of God this is the greatest truth in life.

Love endures all kinds of tests.

A man only thinks when he is loved.

Where Love is - hate vanishes.

Only Love reveals the invisible world.

Pure love gives Divine life.

Love doesn't bear any laws.

True love exists between kindred souls.
God hides his good from those who have no
Love.

The deeper love is, the deeper knowledge is.

Love always succeeds.

He who pins his faith on Love - always wins.

Divine Love is absolute freedom.

Love is wisdom itself.

Love is always active - all space bows before
Love.

Love that is not calming you - is not Divine love.

Whatever advice gives you Love, wisdom and
truth, do it.

Speak the truth to keep Love's way open.

Love of God makes a man strong.

Love shows itself in harmony.

Everything that is not based on Love will vanish.

When you listen with love, you always
understand something.
Love incites the man to work.

Paradise is a place of clean, unselfish, and great
love.

Only Love saves the man from the death.

The subject of Love is purity. Where there is
Love, purity definitely will be there.

Love is something completely spiritual; it is not
something that we can touch.

If you in your thoughts, wishes and actions do
not have purity; if you are not pure, then where
is your love? We have to have and physical, and
spiritual, and Divine purity.

God opens your heart for a definite love.

When Love enters man, the whole world has
another appearance to him.

The true man goes hungry internally for Love.

Love will give you the needed light to understand the meaning of life.

If you do not have Love, Mother Nature is closed for you.

He who loves eats the best food.

Outside the realm of Love, man becomes stranger in this and the other world.

The heart is built according to Love's law.

Everything made with love is blessed.

He who dies for Love - enters a higher world.

Only with Love will you be helped from above.

Love brings in strength, health, and life in man.

Where Love is, there also is justice and security.

The voice gives out love, peace, and the inner life of a man.

Love consists of pure thought.

Love is the most ethereal world.

Where there is no love, sickness and the devil settle.
Love is the very Divine life.

Vegetarian food is Love's food.

Love is a great alchemical law.

Only Love can educate you.
Love dominates everywhere.

Love creates supernatural presence.
If you act everywhere with love, you are invulnerable.

Say "Love" with holiness and purity in your voice.
To see Love, the Good this is the greatest magic.

Love sees only the positive.

Always speak with Love's tone.

When you come to love, the suffering cleans you.
Love reconstructs the cells from human to angelic.

When you love God, everyone will love you.

In Love there are no worries and disturbances.

Love gives out Divine aroma.

It is impossible to love somebody and not to be loved by him.

The eyes are symbols of truth, they never lie. They are man's sky, the soul's certificate. The eyes are the soul's speech.

Out of small things, Love creates precious stones.
Love is in every light thought.

With Love, everything gives out aroma.

There is no place Love does not permeate.

Only Love leads to the truth.

Love seeks the light.

Love must purify you so that nothing negative remains in you.

Love's look is full of life and harmony.

Love beautifies everything.

One's whole future depends on his understanding of Love.

The evil man lives in a constant anxiety. Peace is in Love.
When you believe, believe that you live in the spiritual world.

When you love, you live in the God's world.

The light of the look is the light of Love.

The look reveals the internal world.

All people who are outside of the realm of Love are dead people.
If you can't love a dew drop, you can't love a man too.

The lips are projection of Love.

Love has the quietest voice.

With Love, a man's thought has vibrations that put everything in motion.

The act of every love, wisdom, and truth is due to God, who acts in us.

You can't love a man, in whom God does not act.
When God shows Himself in man, he right away comes to love Him.

What you love comes to you, approaches you.

You have to concentrate in yourself and to seek the beauty.

From Love's spring has derived all the worlds.

Love is this: that which doesn't die, only Love is eternal.

Only God loves, but we are the bearers of his love.

God's love leaves the man free.
God is the only one for Whom you have to sacrifice your life.

He who loves through him passes Divine energy, but he who is loved must take it in.

See Love and all of Its acts with holly excitement, because there God is present.

Love is the only power in the world, for which there are no reverse reactions.

When you have love to God, God blesses you.

When a man loves you, God has fallen in love with you.

Everyone that loves you has impulse from God.

With love coming from God, a man becomes attentive to everybody.

If God loves you, nobody can cause you mischief.

God has created Love, wisdom, and truth.
He who lives with Love renews himself, it is a renewable process.

Do you know about the pulse of a man who is connected with God?
Love of God is golden.

There are things, which only God can resolve.

God is hidden even behind the smallest phenomena.
Karma is liquidated only with the Love law.

If you don't have love, your karma will drag you down.

Break: the spirit comes out of the body, out of the Earth zone, gets renewed, and comes back into the body.

Only God will teach us how to love people.

Love is food for the brain.

God tests us how much we love him.

Love is full of wealth and beauty.
Love has such fine nuances, that words are
weak to express them.

Isn't it Love that carries us in space?

Love excludes all negative actions.

God blesses every act of Love.

Love is in the consciousness of all beings
according to their degree of evolution.

If you want to know whether Love acts in you,
you have to check if you have purity, not just
physical, but also spiritual and Divine.

Love is an act to God, but not to the people.
As you love a man, you love the God in him.

Evil melts before Love.

Everything abnormal is outside of the Divine
love environment.

In your love to God - you free yourself.

He who bears the Love in himself communicates with reasonable beings in an inner way.

Love, wisdom, and truth are the essence of God.

Love is deaf for all bad things.

Love gives value to everything.

When you come out of the realm of Love, you enter suffering.

When you are loved by man - God loves you. If you work with love, God and Mother Nature will help you.

The belief is a way to Love, but Love is a way to God.

Put purity into your heart and Love will enter it in its fullness.

Without love it's impossible to find God.

When a man loves - he shows the God in himself.

Mother Nature has a special goodwill to those who live in Love.

Love is God's visit.

Spirit: that is Love - that is God's manifestation.

Love is perfect hygiene.

Put love in your heart and Love will come and real life will begin.

Love gives meaning to the knowledge.

The man of Love attracts the nature's powers; he is rich.

The man of Love is rich with magnetism.
Love is Divine science.

If you show love to your enemy, he capitulates.

The love of a man towards others changes God's relations towards this man.

All people, who have no love in themselves - they are dead people.

Love resolves all contradictions.

You can't love if God is not inside you.

Love is the only power that connects us with God.

Only with Love's eyes can it be seen clearly.

Love is the rise of the spirit.

Love has a solemn expression which can never get lost.

He, who shows Love, serves God.

Love is a contact of the spirit with God.

Suffering changes to love.

Love is the only power that brings immortality.

Love is a light that comes out of God.

The greatest capital is - love to God.

You will see God in the showings of Love.

For Love everything is nice, for hate everything is bad.

How great is God, He left the soul itself to start longing for Love and return to its homeland.

Love is above everything - it is eternal.

The love of God resolves all problems.

As long as you have love to God - everything will go well.

Love has the nicest speech.

When you love somebody, God takes part in it.

Love, which doesn't make man free, is not love.

Only the love of God melts the karma.

The light talks quietly because it bears the Love in itself.

Only the loving one can see.

A man's love is constantly tested.

Without love of God - there is no conscious life.

Love transforms everything into good.

Knowledge comes always through Love.

The right thought depends on Love.

Love is a light which comes out of God.

All capital is in Love.

The God's kingdom is in the heart of those who love God.

Love treats everyone equally.

Love is that attitude when one sees God in every being.

The greater the man's love is, the more the critics and the spiteful vanish.

Love bathes the man with streams of light.

Love's connection never discontinues, it proceeds even after death.

Outside of Love, karma acts.

If you see love in you - you'll see it in others too.

God stretches his hands to those who correctly show their love.

The love, which is among the souls today, is determined from the former existence.

Every work with love increases the energy. If there is love in something it is blessed.

Only Love can counteract hate.

When you have the smallest negative thought, Love disappears.

All goodness comes from Love.

A man who bears Love, doesn't give in to temptations.

The impatience is with weak love.

He who loves gets a bright face.

Love transforms all powers.

He who loves always gains.

You can love only that being who widens your consciousness.
Love energy can be thickened and can be transformed into light.

If you have love in you, you have to deliver it to others.

Magnetism is a symbol of Love.

He who doesn't serve Love doesn't have a future.

Love that murmurs is not love.

A real man is only that man who comes from Love.

A man of Love can never be unhappy.

Real Love gives one a bright face.

Love must flow in you.

To be loved in a human way - that means to be consumed.

With Love, you are surrounded by all bright spirits.

The only thing that can calm man is Love.

He, who goes away from Love, brings suffering on himself. He who comes near it brings joy on himself.
In moving away from Love comes a bad life.

Love is full of life.

Love is the power, to which nothing can contradict.

Love is seeing the Divine in man, flowers, and animals.

A man of Love gives something nice in others.

Become servants to Love and you'll enter the kingdom of joy.

Every work done with love is a holy work.

When Love looks at you - you melt down.

Love fills every being with joy. Man's soul is woven from Love's rays.

In man you can doubt, but in Love you cannot.

Let's leave Love to speak - it is being radiated.

There is love and life in that which constantly renews.

The flower's love is a fragrance and silence.

He who loves cannot be hurt.
Love creates aura. When you love, the aura becomes stronger.

Only in Love one is rich.

Love is the basic essence of the genesis.

With love everything is open, the ways are clean.

Only Love reveals the life's secrets.

Love brings light to the mind and warmth to the heart.

The ways of God's Love are filled with light.

When Love comes divided - it won't withstand itself.

Love shows itself only through the good.

When Love is being shown in man, he sees only great and lofty things.

The soul is Love's place.

People become old because they are outside of Love.

Love gives meaning to knowledge.
A human's love kills, but the Divine Love resurrects.

God never speaks about his love.

Life in Love is the very perfection.

There is love only then when the persuasion of man is complete.

Love builds real relations.

If you perceive Love, peace, joy, and gaiety will come.

Love is always for the good of others.

Love connects the people's souls.

In Love everyone wins, in hate everyone loses.

He who appreciates Love, it itself comes to him.

People of Love have such radiation, that they can never be forgotten.

In the Divine Love there is always enlargement.

There are contradictions, when Love is being denied.

A man is whatever his love, thought, and belief are.

He, who doesn't go by the Love law, has no future.

Love makes the eyes light and clear.

The knowing of Love gives birth to the immortality.

He, who knows Love, achieves everything.

Love is the foundation of knowledge.

Love comes through suffering.

Love is a passport for returning back to paradise.

Lofty Love is born through abundant internal light.

Love smells sweet everywhere. In Love is the future.

Love has a radiant image.

Love – is lofty like God.

Live in Love and Love will live in you.
Love penetrates into the invisible world.

From Love's eyes emanate a soft, pleasant light.

Love has the most organized eyes.

High Love doesn't wish, it has everything in it.

Love is in the Divine world, but in the man's is only its shade.

Without Love, life remains incomprehensible.

Love puts in order everything, straightens out everything.

He who wants to be resurrected must put Love into practice.

When you easily overcome difficulties, it means you have love.

From the mouth is heard one's love.

One can't comprehend Love, until the idea of God becomes clear to him.

Seek Love inside you, but not outside.

Belief is a quality of Love.

Love is able to realize all conditions and wishes of man.

Love is an absolutely unknown area for the devil.

Love doesn't bear any human order.

Where Love is, there knowledge is.

Only Love bears in itself the great life.

Love is a merging among souls.
Man has aspiration to Love, so that it gives him life.

If you understand Love, life begins to flow in you.

Put more love in you, and things will be all right.

Love has not been seen because of its loftiness.

Love is a power that can endure the greatest suffering.

Loving is the only thing that is immortal.

Where Love is, there old age does not exist.

He who lives in Love is free.
Love hides in itself the knowledge of the whole world.

Joy, happiness, success - come from work only, from the love that you have put in.

Love can make happen all of man's wishes.

Think that God is near by you, and He really will be.

He who genuinely loves God is always optimistic.

Discontent is a lack of love.

Love that changes is not real love.

As long as Love is with you - you are safe.

If you count on another's love you are lost.

Love is the healthiest condition.

Do not go to dangerous places without love.

Only through Love can you travel to all worlds.

When a man criticizes, he destroys the love in himself, and it leaves him.

Only Love can make changes in man's internal life.

You have to love and respect each other not externally, but in an inner way.

When you reveal your love you always lose it.

Only when a man has humility - then the sky will let Love's current run through him.

When you are scared of something, your love is small.

Love centered to God, takes the highest place in a man's head.

When you are scared of something, your love is small.

Love of anybody - is a hidden love of God.

Human love always ends with unhappiness, there are no exemptions here.

Love, wisdom, and truth are unchanging centers, around which the whole universe rotates.

In the Love world there is nothing negative.

Love only is that thing which doesn't lose its beauty.

Love stands above every thought and glory.

The love of a certain fruit improves its quality. Love liquidates karma.

Love takes down the chains from the mind and the heart.

When Hate meets Love, Hate right away capitulates.

Love has positive thoughts.
The seraphs - their aims are woven of love.

Love is like sunlight.

Every day: intensive Love life.

If you are armed with Love, no one would push you.

Love never sees mistakes.

In Love everything is nice.

There is no Love in the coward.

Where Love is, everything can be achieved.

One's self is the real sacrifice for Love.

The man's love is determined by how much he cares for his soul.

Where Love is, there the success is.

He who loves becomes great.

He who loves sees God.

41

Love that retreats before obstacles is not a real love.

There is no atom, ion or molecule that doesn't contain Love energy.

The reason of life is in Love; do everything with love.

The flip side of hate is again love, dressed in somebody else's garment, with the goal to test what is hidden in your heart.

Defeat evil with love.

Love forgives but doesn't excuse.

When reasonable beings want to talk about Love, they send their energies to the man's heart, below the pit of the stomach, or to the top part of his brain - these are three kinds of senses.

Accept Love: in you in order for God to help you.

Only he loves who has overgrown the physical conditions, and who is master of himself.

If an unclean thought enters your mind, put it right away in the God's Love fire, to burn up and turn to ashes.

Live there, where Love is.

When you lose Love, you lose also the benefits that it brings.

Man's freedom is determined by his love, wisdom, and truth applied.

With Love, life is paradise and bliss.
Where Love is, there everything is pleasant.

Man must be ready to do good anywhere, to know that the world is a holy school, where God is manifesting Himself.

The man of Love is a master of death, and all mean and negative powers of the world.

Where Love is, there old age doesn't exist - in old age we understand the absence of love.

The greatest thing in the world is Love.

Love can change the world.

Apply Love even in the smallest work.

He who lives in Love is free.
When you finish your spiritual development, you acquire Love.

He, who goes in directions opposite to the Love, gradually loses his health and strength.

If you give with love - you'll be gifted with love, too.

If it's about the love, seek for the God's Love.

Love that changes is not real.

In general, a man who has love and aspiration to God can be helped by having such.

If your life becomes meaningless, you are far away from Love.

Only he who loves truly produces joy in the souls of his associates.

The accessible thing is the Love, and when it enters man, it rejuvenates and raises him.

The loving is immortal.

While Love is with you, you are safe. When it leaves you, you drown.

Love brings the new in the world - look for it and it will renew you - that relates to God's love.

Where the light and the warmth is, there Love is.

He who lives in Love, cannot burn up. - Why? - He is dressed with the Love garment, which doesn't burn.

Love - the great life law that acts on Earth and in Heaven.

Where the conscious takes part - there things happen with Love.

The more responsive and open to Love one is, the more it reveals itself to him.

Who can love? - Only the smart and good man is able to love.

If you are faithful to Love, in this and your next life you will benefit from the benefits that it brings.

The accessible thing is the Love, and when it enters man, it rejuvenates and raises him up.

The loving is immortal.

While Love is with you, you are safe. When it leaves you, you drown.

Love brings the new in the world - look for it and it will renew you - that relates to God's love.

Where the light and the warmth is, there Love is.

He who lives in Love, cannot burn up. - Why? - He is dressed in the Love garment, which doesn't burn.

Love - the great life law that acts on Earth and in Heaven.

Where the consciousness takes part - there things happen with Love.

The more responsive and open to Love one is, the more it reveals itself to him.

Who can love? - Only the smart and good man is able to love.

If you are faithful to Love, in this and your next life you will benefit from the benefits that it brings.

The way to Love is open; he who wants to can freely go along that way.

A big secret is hidden in the God's Love.

I wish you to accept the God's Love, and to travel with it within all worlds.

Put Love as the foundation in your life. In it are hidden conditions and possibilities for health, happiness and success.

Where Love misses, there everything is deprived from content and beauty.

In Love, disease does not exist. The loving man is a healthy, strong, and powerful man.

If you get connect with Love, the joy will come, which will bring you happiness.

Why is a man dissatisfied? - Because he doesn't bear the Love in his soul.

Every movement has meaning when it is fulfilled with love.

If you apply Love, you already have entered into paradise in the Divine world.

What is Love? - building power in life and nature.

The foundation of every Divine teaching is Love.

If you want to be healthy, strong, and calm, you have to love.

He who has love in himself; he is always clean, washed, and dressed.

Remember: The Divine teaching is locked up in love to God.

Love is passed through a teacher.
Love defeats all difficulties. Love awakens the Divine in man.

When you come upon Love, know that, all loving souls are connected with lofty and reasonable beings from the invisible world.
If you acquire Love, you acquire the help of thousands and millions souls. Under love is understood collective work of numerous souls, united in one idea, in one understanding.

Love comes from something that is constant and unchangeable.

Love is not to be touched, it must be watched only from afar, it bears no touching.

Love brings meaning to life. It presents the reasonable beginning, which comes out of God.

God created the world to show Love.

In the world of Love there is nothing negative.

Put Love as an armor against the evils of the world.

Every lofty and noble thing comes from Love.

He, who lives in Love, is debt free.

You can't find God without Love.

Believe in Love, it always employs the truth. Love does not stay with sinners.

All diseases, infirmities, sorrows, are cured with Love.

Knowledge without love brings unhappiness. Knowledge with love brings blessings.

To accept the Love for yourself and keep it clean as it comes from God, this thing we call "love".

Life born from Love brings happiness.

Even the biggest evil retreats before Love.

Love paralyzes the action of all poisons.
There is no power in the world, which can oppose Love; it is a cure for all diseases, armor against all poisons and evils.

Eat and drink always with love, so that you can be healthy. Eat without overeating and thank God for the food.

Where Love is, there comes help; where there is no love, there is no help either.

He, who bears the Love in his soul, communicates with reasonable beings in an inner way.

This, which is not told about Love, is the true Love.

When your life starts getting well, then is enacted the Love law.
Love excludes death, discouragement, and suffering.

Love is an ascending process; on that account it is occupied with great things.

If Mother Nature has love towards you, she herself will confide her secrets to you.

Which is the real wealth? - God's Love, the Divine knowledge, and God's truth - They follow man to the other world too.

He who knows Love, talks about God's greatness, not about his own.

How will the world be set right? - Through the Love fire.
- The strongest fire that exists in the whole universe is the Love fire.
Wherever that fire is directed, it melts everything.

It is a great benefit for the soul to pass through the Love fire.
The whole universe will open for you, as a dwelling; you will feel your connection with God, as your father.

The connection between souls is Love.

Love brings life, strength, and light; it is life's foundation.

What is wanted from a man, in order to preach?
- Love.

He, who has acquired Love, easily copes with life's sufferings.
- If there is no love, the sufferings turn to torture.

The Love connects the beings from the physical world, with those from the spiritual and mental world. It is not enough to see those beings - it is important to hear their speech. - When you find yourself in difficulty, they begin to whisper something to you - listen attentively to their talk and do what they say.

Love is a power that can bear the whole universe.

Love cleans everything. When a man goes to God, he cleans himself out.

Nowadays, a man is not ready yet to accept Love directly, with all of its strength and fullness.

If you don't have love, your knowledge is worth nothing.

The only power that doesn't lose its balance is Love.
Put on one side of the scales, it is balanced with all powers of the world.

If your love doesn't change, you really have love.

Where Love is, there is a light.

Freedom is determined by Love - only the loving can be free.

He, who really loves you, leaves you free.
When you love, you leave him free too.

Love is a law, through which all reasonable wishes are achieved.

The first quality of Love is reasonableness.

He who loves is reasonable; he treats carefully those whom he loves.

All evil things and crimes occur outside of Love.

Love comes out of God, but through the people who Love.

He, who lives in Love, cannot make mistakes.

He, who enters into temptation, is outside of Love, out of the real life.

Apply Love, in order to understand the law of unity.

He, who lives in Love, has his things set right.

Why does a man suffer? - In order to be tested in his love and stability.

As long as one bears the ordinary love in himself, he always will die.

The light shows itself only by Love.

Remember: Without God, i.e. without Love, there is no life.

There are two ways for a man to be set right: Law and Love.

Everything done without love disappears.

Listen to the voice of reason in you, this voice is the Love voice.

In life, Love is the basic tone.
- Without the basic tone, a man is in the dark.

Love is the law of coming near:
- The physical closeness, by itself, doesn't have
a relation to Love.

There is no other way except Love. It reveals all
secrets.

He, who has acquired the Love, has already
aspired to life happiness.

Only Love is in the condition to solve your
difficulties.
Love is the way for solving one's tough problems
in his life.

One falls only when he has no love in himself.

Everything that has passed through the door
of Love, wisdom, and truth, has acquired
immortality.

The unhappiness comes, when one breaks off
his connection with Love, wisdom, and truth.

Love is the rock with which everything gets
broken.

What is Love? - Love is a world of favors.

Love is a world of abundance - all goodness is in its hands.

Love is the greatest capital.

A cold man cannot be loved, because people love warmth.

There must be something unearthly in Love.

Love will transform you to light.

When you come to love with somebody, ask yourself if that love comes from God, or from somewhere else.

Everything that happens to those who love God is for their benefit.

The bad thoughts go back only before Love.

If you enter in Love - everything unclean comes out.

Before the great God's Love, everything retreats.

In God only there is fullness of joy and love.

The Divine life requires permanently living in Love.

In the love to God there are no losses.

The real prayer is expressed through Love.

He who has a heart full with love eternally rejuvenates himself.

Human's love is a swamp, but the Divine is a spring.

Your love must be a current to the people.
If one doesn't know Love, he cannot think rightly.

Only Love can connect you with lofty beings.

The angel is a great servant to Love: the angel is love.

Have love for the angels and they will reveal themselves to you.

With Love, the angels are always with you.

Loving is extremely foreseeing.
It can be spoken without love in humans' language, but not in angels'.

The angels can't be without love. They feed themselves with love.

The angels have only one ideal - eternal love.

A world, in which Love is absent, is a world of death.
Love is a world of immortality.

To all who work honestly and truly, God will reveal his love.

Only God is He who reveals the truth in the world.

There is no greater good for a man than this to love all people.

The angels have found Love – that is why they are up.

Love, for the angels is a holy world.

When an angel enters man, man acquires cosmic love.
Angels live in the Love world; where Love is, there the abundance is.
In Love there are never privations.

Happiness means connection with Love,
connection with God.

Clean love and clean truth are the food in the
Divine world.
Anything unclean is outside of the Divine world.

He, who loves, has light, with which he sees.

Love dominates above all worlds.

Love for the pure people never gets lost. It
eternally gives warmth.

The most beautiful things are outside of time
and space.
The bright thoughts are only part of the great
God's love.

He who doesn't bear the great Love idea in
himself -
cannot exalt himself to the lofty world.

That's why the devil is sent, if you don't love -
he will torture you, and you will suffer.

Everything, done with love brings in pure
vitality.

If you have rejected Love, there is old age, sickness, and contradictions.

For the angel, only Love is important, for only Love ensures.

Let Love into you and it will clean you up.

Love is a light; it sees everything and throws light upon everything.

For the man of Love - the difficulties bring goodness.

The clean love melts all karmic connections.

Constantly seek Love and it will take you to God.

Love is the greatest wealth in the world.

Love is a law for finding the truth.

The light thoughts lead to Love.

Only Love ensures the future.

Love is the most satisfied world, for God is in it.

With Love you enter in the hidden world of God.

He who is with clean life and has found Love
- he doesn't ask what is the meaning of life.

Everything depends on that how deep your love
is.

Love has transformative power.
Perfect is only the spirit, but Love is its
expression.

Enter deeply in the God's Love; it is out of all
negative conditions.

Whoever doesn't tolerate Love is full of hate.

When you love only, you see the Divine world.

He who loves, through him flow the Divine
energies of the paradise.

Only the clean man can love.

Without love - there is no health.
Where Love is, there the diseases leave.

Love is an armor against all diseases.

The diseases show, that Love has left the man.

Love is the most perfect thought.

With all your thoughts, serve Love.

Every thought, deprived of love, has no strength.
Above the world is the thought, above the thought is Love.

Only through Love does one come back to life.

Within the relations of others, see God, Who acts.

Clear thought is an expression of Love.

When a thought lights up in your mind, Love has come.

When you think about Love, all bad thoughts flee.

A thought, that is full of love, moves a long distance.

Love has alchemic properties, which can transform.

Divine Love is an occult. It is the life center.

When you love only one being, you fence them in.

Thought is a great principle, which is contained in God.
Love surpasses every thought.

Where Love is, there are nice thoughts and feelings.

He, who loves, thinks right.
Every thought submits to Love.

When you think about Love, you should enter into it.

For Love, there are no problems.

Love is a power, for it is a God's law.

Love is the greatest wealth in the world.

Where Love is present, there abundance lies.

Love is a mighty power.

He who loves is a strong spirit.

Love must be studied as a live power.

From the eyes and the hands, life must come out.

Everything bows down and retreats before Love.

Love is God's power.
If a man enters Love's realm, he enters the
Divine world.

Love achieves everything.
In order to know Love, you have to put it into
practice.

Apply Love even in the smallest things.

Love - that is a great liberation.

Love swallows up all problems and obstacles.

Love is a power from which all problems flee.

The most supreme love is that which is not
expressed with words.

When you think about the Love, all bad
thoughts flee.

The inner voice talks in Love's name.

Love is a rock, with which everything (negative)
is destroyed.

Wish deeply in your soul for Love to your being.

When Love burns internally, it is transmitted to others.

Live in Love and all the benefits are in your hands.

Love reaches the bottom of all things.

Be with Love in order for it to be with you.

The clean thought is a statement of Love.

Whatever a man's love is, that is his thought.

Showing Love is serving God.

God is He who gives orders for everything.

Where Love is, everything is well arranged.

The one who really loves is absolutely secured.

He, who bears Love, is from the chosen.

Love contains all kinds of methods for renewal.

Love gives meaning to every detail.

Light thoughts strengthen the love in man.

The formula - God is Love contains God's kingdom in itself.

When you live in Love, it gives you all favorable conditions.

The Divine opens itself its own way.

Love is outside of one's thoughts, feelings, and actions.

When Love is in you, everything is nice.
With Love, you are secured for lifetime.

Love is a great creative power.

When one stays in your thoughts, you love him.

God's Love produces only positive thoughts.

Love seeks people with strong thoughts.

When you apply Love, it becomes understood.

Love is far away from the human world.

God's power radiates from Love.

Love is Divine magnetism.

Love is the temple of God.

God's Love arranges our future more securely
than any insurance
company.

Only Love assures peace and eternal life.

Only Love raises man up.

All secrets are hidden in Love.

In everything that you love, God shows himself.
Love of God has to be above everything.

The beautiful look is always the look of Love.

Seek first Love and everything else will be given
to you.

Where Love enters, the benefits come in flocks.

Where Love is, there are achievements.

There is something better than to love; it is to
become love.

Love must fill the air.

If you want to be rich, you have to love
somebody.

Love comes out from bright seeing.

Every being that you love will appear to you.

Only he who loves can show his genuine nature.

Only with Love will the mind function rightly.

Love is superior to happiness - Love includes it.
Love is immunized from all diseases.
If we have love - the diseases vanish.

Love is a sunny state of the mind and the heart.

Only that thing which has been accomplished
with love will remain.

When Love gets restricted in man, the truth also
gets restricted.

Love is directed by intelligent beings with
finished development.

Love is the shortest way to the truth.

Love can enlarge you so much, that you fall in
love with the whole world.

Calmness is the wealth of Love.

Only through Love can someone be more than
himself.

Where there is no love, there is no truth.

Love surpasses every kind of knowledge.

True love is to forget about yourself.

When there is no love, there are crooked thoughts.

What sleeping is deeper than this: for one to deny Love. The tender voice is part of Love.

Love never goes astray - people do.

Only Love knows who loves it.

When you give something with love, that which is given increases in you.

A strong man is the one who loves without expectation to be loved.

Love is the happiest viewpoint.

Only two things hint about the other world - Love and the religion.

The whole reasonable world is present in Love.

Outside of Love there are no achievements.

If you talk about people's mistakes, you are far away from Love.

Purity makes man receptive to the lofty Love vibrations.

There is no soul that does not respond to the Divine love.

True love forgives everything.

Where there is no love, life goes into distraction.

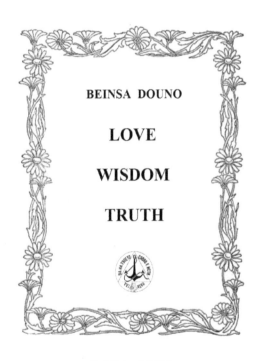

BEINSA DOUNO

LOVE

WISDOM

TRUTH

Published 2011.
Available on amazon.com.

Made in the USA
Middletown, DE
01 August 2023

36017258R00046